GUIDING LIGHTS
Lighthouses

Peter Ashley

Everyman Pocket Books
In association with English Heritage

Lantern Room at **North Foreland, Kent**
(p. 1)

Dovercourt, Essex Stunning eyecatchers,
these lights relieve the monotony of an
otherwise dull seafront, with rusted sea legs and
sawn-off staircases, turrets of cast-iron plates,
and on the High light a creaking weathervane
pierced with the date 1862.
(p. 2)

Guiding Lights – Lighthouses

**Published by Everyman Publishers Plc
in association with English Heritage**

© 2001 Everyman Publishers Plc
Text and photographs © Peter Ashley

ISBN 1 84159 046 0

Design by Anikst Design
Printed in Singapore

Everyman Publishers Plc
Gloucester Mansions
140a Shaftesbury Avenue
London WC2H 8HD

In the middle of photography for this book,
Britain was hit by the terrible scourge of foot-
and-mouth disease. Many lighthouses were
rendered out of bounds, access only being
restored in the very final stages of production.
Two that would certainly have been included
were Tater Du in Cornwall and Start Point in
Devon. They were still cut off by restrictions
at the time of going to press, but may be
included in any later editions.

contents

introduction *The thin tongue of coast was so flat that it was like a scar on the sea. Nothing rose above the level of the one-storeyed shacks scattered about it like cubes of sea-worn wreckage except a lighthouse, standing up like a vast white candle in a wide lofty sky, so that from a distance it seemed to float in air.* The Lighthouse, H.E.Bates

James looked at the lighthouse. He could see the white-washed rocks; the tower, stark and straight; he could see that it was barred with black and white; he could see windows in it; he could even see the washing spread on the rocks to dry. So that was the Lighthouse, was it? To the Lighthouse, Virginia Woolf

They are functional, but they are something else as well. They have strength, gaiety of design and colour.... and they are usually in stark contrast with their surroundings. Buildings and Prospects, John Piper

We are as familiar with lighthouses as we are with church towers. Soaring above us, they capture the imagination as well as the eye. They share a common history, with beacons on churches often being used to guide seafarers, as at Happisburgh and Cromer, and inland travellers guided in their struggles across the Fens to Ely or through the Rockingham Forest. Now it is the towering lighthouses on cliffs, headlands and shingle spits that are the guiding lights to mariners, warning them of the perils of the coastline or safely gathering them into havens and harbours.

Most lighthouses were originally erected by shipowners and corporations, but gradually they came under the authority of Trinity House, which currently maintains 72 lighthouses in the UK, all now fully automated.

Trinity House has worked continually since the reign of Henry VIII in maritime pilotage, although it was not until 1609 that they built their first lighthouse in Lowestoft. Centuries of folklore, romance and heroism came to an end in November 1998 when the last keepers left the North Foreland Lighthouse in Kent, and it went over to automatic operation. So I was too late to photograph the very human aspect of lighthouse keeping. Although it was very obviously a job with great technical responsibility, life on a lighthouse offered unique aspects of domestic living. A bizarre example is folding sheets with special tucks and creases so that they snugly fitted the curved beds against circular walls.

This is not a technical book. There are many sources to indulge those keen on the optical characteristics of first order catadioptric fixed lenses, but this is simply a tour of the English mainland coast from Northumberland to Cumbria, looking at a selection of lighthouses and navigational aids in the landscape and recounting anecdotes picked up on the way. Many are listed buildings, and we should all be grateful to English Heritage for their commitment to our built environment, which preserves these wonderfully evocative structures for future generations. In a book of this size we've had to be very selective, and offshore lights that require boat or helicopter rental to see them have had to be excluded. But at least it means that, in general, every location is very easily accessible.

There are many unsung lights and beacons here, particularly in little harbours and at the end of lonely jetties. More than perhaps any other building, their visual appeal arises directly from their function, so I shall never forget my first sighting of the wonderful red Martian welcoming a ship into the Tyne at South Shields. I hope they all give you as much pleasure.

the north east

Berwick-on-Tweed, Northumberland The first (or last) lighthouse in England. This most northerly light was built as the finishing touch to the long jetty in the early 1820s. Originally the light in this red-capped tower of local stone was run from large, unwieldy batteries charged up in a garage in the town. The charge lasted a week, and Friday was set aside to trundle the renewed batteries on a wheelbarrow out from the town and on to the jetty – almost a day's work. In Berwick they still talk of the time when two chaps assigned with this task arrived exhausted at the light, each believing that the other had the key.

Bamburgh, Northumberland Peeping like a friendly face over the dunes is the Bamburgh sector light. Built here within sight of the dramatic castle in 1910, it guides vessels navigating around the Farne Islands. In the late 18th century an appropriately named Dr. Sharp kept an eye on this stretch of coast from the ramparts of Bamburgh Castle, operating a noisy system of bells and guns, and sending out riders during gales to watch for ships in distress.

Seahouses, Northumberland A thoroughly workman-like harbour from where, in the summer months, you can take a boat out to the Farne Islands. The little salt cellar of a light sits at the end of a pier filled with boats pulled up for maintenance, lobster and crab creels, and divers struggling to attach themselves to yellow air tanks.

Blyth, Northumberland A rusting light sits far out on its mile long pier, sharing the elements with a row of wind turbines. Blyth was once a busy port exporting coal, and one of the first English railways consisting of horses drawing wagons along parallel beams of wood brought coal from Bebside colliery to the harbour.

St. Mary's Island, Tyne & Wear Whitley Bay is where Newcastle comes to the seaside. At the north end of the beach is the sandstone St. Mary's Island, sometimes known as Bait Island, reached at low tide over a causeway through rocks strewn with seaweed and sand. The 126-foot lighthouse and keepers' cottages were built here in 1898 by the John Miller company of Tynemouth, using 645 blocks of Heworth stone and 750,000 bricks, at a cost of £8,000. They stand on the site of a monastic cell, where the sanctuary light would have acted as a guide to passing vessels.

The Groin, South Shields, Tyne & Wear A Wellsian Martian stands in white plimsolls at the end of the Groin, facing the mouth of the Tyne. It was built by the Newcastle Trinity House Board in 1880, and in lighthouse parlance 'exhibited' its light for the first time on 30th October 1882. This is a wonderfully bright and airy spot on a kind day, with a view across the river to Tynemouth Priory and Castle, but when the famous Tyne fog shrouds the tower, a bell behind the white railings tolls out a warning once every five seconds.

∧ **Roker, Tyne & Wear** This 50-foot wrought-iron tower once braved the elements on the South Pier at Sunderland. It now stands in peaceful retirement on the lawns of Cliff Park in Roker, moved here in 1983 when the pier was shortened to improve access to the Tyne.

< **Souter Point, Whitburn, Tyne & Wear** The currents of the aptly named Whitburn Steel have brought about the wrecking of many ships. High on the rocks above Marsden Bay is the first lighthouse to be reliably lit by electricity. At 75 feet high, the 1871 Souter light was one of the most advanced in the world. Now in the care of the National Trust, it provides a very satisfying opportunity to see how lighthouses work.

∧ **Hartlepool** The original 1846 gas-fuelled light on the Hartlepool Headland was removed in 1915 to allow the nearby Heugh gun battery an uninterrupted view of the North Sea. This 1926 steel replacement stands with its guardian cannon on the original site.

> Down on the Old Pier is a deceptively modern looking lighthouse, an illusion greatly helped by the revolving radar scanner. It is in fact a beacon carried on what was once an open wooden frame, now boarded over.

South Gare Breakwater, Redcar & Cleveland This little light belongs to the Tees & Hartlepool Port Authority, and can be seen for a considerable distance over the muddy, inhospitable flats that continue out to the mouth of the Tees from the huge smoky pall of the steelworks at Redcar. The end of the breakwater, made from ironwork slag and concrete, is in fact a very dangerous place, and should be approached with extreme caution, if at all. The 1884 lighthouse was designed by John Fowler in cast iron with a copper dome that, until 1980, sprouted a chimney and weathervane. The road there passes a little harbour filled with small boats with names like 'Odin', a marine club with the word 'CAFE' painted in huge letters on the roof, and a red corrugated-iron lifeboat station.

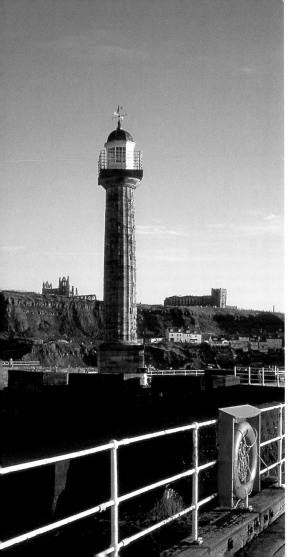

Whitby, North Yorkshire

The quintessential English harbour town, with the River Esk finally reaching the sea from the North Yorkshire moors. The red roofed houses and herring smokeries tumble down the east cliff from the wind blasted churchyard of St. Mary's and the jagged ruins of the abbey. A local architect, Francis Pickernell, designed the 83-foot west lighthouse in 1835, topping his fluted Greek Doric column with an octagonal lantern. The east light is 54 feet high, built in 1855 and redundant since a red light was inserted into the steps of the parish church.

Whitby, North Yorkshire These wooden-legged beacons can be found at the end of the two jetties that form the entrance to the harbour. The high land behind the east beacon is Ling Hill, home to the Whitby Low Light on the following page. A late afternoon stroll down the west jetty, in the sun with a strong breeze blowing, is one of the best 'English Jetty Experiences' I know.

Whitby Low Light, North Yorkshire This light on Ling Hill appears to hang on to the cliffs by its fingertips. Access is restricted, so it can really only be seen from the Cleveland Way that passes above it. A combination of a fast surging high tide, an uneven sea bed and hazardous rocks within a few miles resulted in Trinity House building a pair of towers here in 1858. In 1890 a more efficient light was installed and one tower was taken down. It now sits between two keepers' houses and was finally automated in 1992.

Flamborough Head, East Riding of Yorkshire The great headland at Flamborough reaches out into the sea, north of Bridlington – a chalky extension of the Yorkshire Wolds. Approaching the village, the road passes the Old Tower, which was built in 1674 by Sir John Clayton, but never lit.

Flamborough Head, East Riding of Yorkshire The present 185-foot lighthouse with its 29-mile beam has withstood the storms and withering blasts of this Yorkshire coast since 1806, a waypoint for coastal traffic and a headland marker for vessels approaching Scarborough and Bridlington. In 1998 Trinity House installed a Differential Global Positioning System, (thankfully abbreviated to a DGPS station), which, with six others, gives overlapping coverage of up to fifty sea miles around the coast.

Withernsea, East Riding of Yorkshire The Withernsea lighthouse pops up from amongst the houses like a monstrous garden ornament. Its handsome tapering octagonal column, built to tower over the town in 1892, is now a museum demonstrating the work of both the Royal National Lifeboat Institute and HM Coastguard. The lamp room is attained by climbing up 144 steps, but the views across Holderness and this East Yorkshire seaside town are well worth the exertion.

Spurn Head, East Riding of Yorkshire East of Hull, the Plain of Holderness thins into a clawing finger, beckoning into the Humber estuary. This is Spurn Head, three miles long, occasionally only thirty feet wide, and possibly the only place in England where it's possible to walk from a northwest coast to a southeast coast in seconds. The peninsula is the result of immense coastal erosion to the north, the material being dragged down and deposited by the tides. The beaches are patterned with bright orange, smooth bricks from lost buildings. Two lighthouses can be found just as the spit starts to widen at the tip that is home to the country's only full-time lifeboat crew.

< The column of the old low light now supports a bird-haunted water tank on the edge of the waves that once supplied water to the original lighthouse cottages. This brick column was one of two towers built here by the Eddystone lighthouse engineer, John Smeaton, in 1776.

∧ The high light forlornly straddles the dunes, abandoned in 1985. It still acts as a daymark amongst mud-filled channels with evocative names like 'Old Den' and 'Greedy Gut'.

east anglia

‹ **Guy's Head, Sutton Bridge, Lincolnshire** Shipping and the pilot boat are the most frequent visitors to this remote spot that only just divides sky from water. Two lighthouses stand where the last of the River Nene slips almost anonymously into The Wash, sentinels built not for navigation but to mark the entrance of the new Nene Channel, opened in 1831. Both are buildings in the Fenland tradition, more like tower windmills with bull's-eye windows set into their sail-less caps. The white painted west lighthouse has also seen service as a Home Guard post in the Second World War and a very useful customs and excise lookout.

ʌ The east lighthouse provided a perfect studio for wildfowl preservationist and painter, Sir Peter Scott, during the 1930s.

<< **Hunstanton, Norfolk** Hunstanton marks
the point where the east coast turns and
curiously faces west across The Wash.
The cliffs here are a geologist's delight, a
layer cake of red chalk, creamy chalk, and
gingerbread carstone. On the clifftop a
sweep of grass contains a ruined arch from
the 13th-century St. Edmund's Chapel, and
the white rendered brick lighthouse of 1830.
Originally there were two adjoining keepers'
houses, but only one survives, converted
in 1964.

< **Cromer, Norfolk** In medieval times,
guidance for vessels was often by beacon
lights on convenient church towers. This
was certainly true at Cromer, on top of the
impressive steeple of St. Peter and St. Paul.
A later lighthouse tower of 1717 provided
light by a coal fire enclosed in a lantern, and
when this was replaced by rapidly flickering
oil lamps, seamen complained of its
stroboscopic effect, calling it a 'will'-o-the-
wisp'. The first two keepers were women,
who shared one pound per week in wages.
After a succession of cliff falls the whole
edifice finally ended up on the beach in
1866. This white octagonal tower dates
from 1833, and is best seen from the
clifftop footpath from Cromer to Overstrand
that passes nearby.

Happisburgh, Norfolk The church of St. Mary in Happisburgh with its 110-foot tower has always been a seamark on this remote curve of Norfolk. In the churchyard the graves of the shipwrecked and the dull boom of the sea are constant reminders of a treacherous coast. Out in the fields stands this glorious red and white striped lighthouse, a true beacon of hope built in 1791.

Lowestoft, Suffolk At the start of the 17th century, shipowners and merchants who were losing vessels on sandbanks and shoals petitioned Trinity House for a high and low light at Lowestoft-ness, for, in their words '...the direction of ships which crept by night in the dangerous passage betwixt Lowestoft and Winterton.' Two towers were built in 1609, using tallow candle lights which, when brought into line, guided shipping through the now extinct Stamford Channel. Over the years a succession of fuels (including whale oil and paraffin), lamps and reflectors were employed until successful experiments with electricity at the South Foreland lighthouse eventually brought a new high light. The tower we see today was completed in 1874. It stands in suburban greenery at the top of one of the steep sets of steps descending the Lowestoft cliffs known as 'The Scores'. The low light was finally extinguished in 1923.

Southwold, Suffolk In the Suffolk edition of the *Buildings of England*, Pevsner describes the Southwold lighthouse as 'benevolent'. And indeed that's how it appears, a kindly light gathering the streets and greens of this toy-coloured seaside town around its base. The Trinity House description is a shining catalogue of the succession of lights used to send the beam out over Sole Bay: '1890...an Argand burner...1906...a Matthews incandescent oil burner...1923...a Hood 100mm petroleum vapour burner.' Electrification and de-manning in 1938 must have brought a sterile silence after all those hot flames and oily aromas.

High & Low Lights, Harwich, Essex Harwich is the home of the Trinity House Operational Control Centre, and in the town are numerous reminders of their services to mariners, including this grounded buoy. Behind it in West Street is the tapering ninety-foot nonagonal High Lighthouse, built in 1818 to a design by the civil engineer, John Rennie, Senior. Before the advent of the electric telegraph, the tower housed a flock of carrier pigeons.

The Low Light is now a Maritine Museum, and shares the seafront with bleached beach huts and the frenetic activity of a children's playground.

inland lighthouses

> **Crich Stand, Derbyshire** Take a tram from the Crich Tramway Museum, and from your toast rack wooden seat as you rattle up through the wood, you will see this lighthouse emerge on top of a jagged cliff. Until 1922 there was a view tower here, built by the Hurts of Aldersley, but after the traumas of the First World War it was replaced by this memorial to the Sherwood Foresters. 11,409 men from this Derbyshire and Nottinghamshire regiment lost their lives in this war alone. The flashing beacon also commemorates those who fell in the Second World War.

∨ **St. Mary's Church, Weldon, Northamptonshire** The original name of the village, 'Weldon in the Woods', gives a clue to the function of this handsome glazed cupola on the tower of St. Mary's church. The lantern was paid for by a grateful traveller who, lost amongst the trees, was guided to safety by the sight of the tower. It became a true guiding light for wayfarers making their sometimes perilous way through the Rockingham Forest, the vast hunting grounds that once covered this northeastern corner of Northamptonshire.

the south east

North Foreland, Kent This white wedding cake lighthouse appears unexpectedly on a bend of the road north of Broadstairs. Neatly trimmed hedges lead up to the perfect grouping of the tower and two keepers' houses. Built in 1691, this was the last Trinity House light to be automated – over 300 years of service with lanterns fuelled by coal (100 tons a year in 1698) oil, and now electricity. The rig attached to the balcony railings is part of an escape mechanism whereby keepers could escape fire by abseiling down the tower by a rope looped through the iron eyes. A unique way of life came to an end on 26 November 1998, when the keepers left more conventionally from the last manned lighthouse in the United Kingdom.

South Foreland, Kent A rough lane leads out of St.Margaret's at Cliffe, winding through the trees to Lighthouse Down. From here is the shortest distance to the coast of France (21 miles) and the 1793 South Foreland lighthouse looks out over the tightly packed shipping lanes. The light no longer sweeps the English Channel, but the white pepper-pot tower still acts as a landmark for ferries entering Dover, for channel swimmers, and for walkers on the Saxon Shore Way that passes just below on the cliff edge. It is in the care of the National Trust.

Dungeness, Kent This 6,000-acre triangle of shingle was formed by two opposing sea currents in the English Channel, and is still growing. This is a strange, solitary land of black-tarred fishermen's huts, bungalows made from Southern Railway carriages and uncompromising plants gripping the salt-swept pebbles. A unique hazard to shipping, there have been lighthouses here since around 1600. The 143-foot high Old Lighthouse was constructed in brick in 1904, one of the highest in the United Kingdom, and painted originally in bold black and white stripes to act as a seamark in daylight hours.

The building of the nuclear power station obscured its light, and in 1961 the current lighthouse was built almost 500 yards to the east. This upturned torch is made from pre-cast rings, with the black stripe colour impregnated into the concrete. The pattern of squares near the top conceals the fog warning equipment.

Beachy Head, East Sussex 'The sun searches out every crevice amongst the grass, nor is there the smallest fragment of surface which is not sweetened by air and light. Underneath, the chalk itself is pure, and the turf thus washed by wind and rain, sun-dried and dew-scented, is a couch prepared with thyme to rest on. Discover some excuse to be up there always...' *The Breeze on Beachy Head*, Richard Jefferies.

'Beau Chef' ('beautiful headland') was the name given to this massive chalk cliff by the Normans, now corrupted over the centuries to 'Beachy'. This is where the South Downs are sheered off abruptly, a 534-foot drop to a rocky beach. Here in 1902 Sir Thomas Matthews, the Trinity House engineer-in-chief, directed the building of the famous lighthouse down on the shore. A cableway constructed on the cliff top lowered 3,660 tons of Cornish granite to where the site was contained within a wave-resisting coffer-dam. The lighthouse endured a narrow escape in 2000, when a not insignificant portion of the cliff decided to collapse over the beach, and in April the following year, a section known as the Devil's Chimney followed it. On the next headland is Belle Tout lighthouse, recently moved back wholesale from the eroding cliff edge.

Newhaven, East Sussex The Sussex Ouse once entered the Channel at Seaford, but in 1579 the river suddenly changed its mind in a storm and flowed out instead at the village of Meeching, later to be called Newhaven. Signs saying 'tenez la gauche' and 'centre ville' tell you that this is a port for France. If you need a further reminder, climb up by Lord Palmerston's fort on the cliffs and listen out for the thunderous ship's horn as the Dieppe ferry is piloted out of the harbour. The jetty was completed in 1891, 3,000 feet of curving stone strung with warnings of the high voltage cables that feed the iron light at its head.

southern england

Hurst Point, Hampshire A shingle spit one and a half miles long loops out from the Hampshire coastline, as if in a desperate attempt to reach the Isle of Wight. It is the mainland, but only just. At its bulbous head is Hurst Castle, with Henry VIII's bastion at its core, and immense Victorian batteries winging off on either side. This is the guardian of the Western Solent, the kind of castle where the past is almost touchable. No irrelevant distractions here; everything, from the monstrous guns with their own railway to bring them ammunition, to the three very different lighthouses, delights the eye with its strength of determined purpose.

Take the passenger ferry from Keyhaven, and as it winds through the yachts straining at anchor, the 1867 white tower lighthouse becomes clearer against the background of the Island. On landing, what had appeared to be fortified turrets reveal themselves as two former lights, breaking the profile of the gargantuan walls of the castle. In 1865 the white granite-walled tower was built on the parapet, and this was replaced in 1911 with what was originally a bright red daymark, gas lit at night. It is now camouflaged in a coat of service grey, but its red top and weathervane are preserved down amongst the batteries. Both were warnings of The Shingles out in the Solent, and the continual shifting of this hazardous sandbank has resulted in adjustable high intensity projectors being installed in 1997 in the High Lighthouse down on the shore.

ˇ **Anvil Point, Dorset** Built of the local stone, Anvil Point lighthouse sits below the downs near Durlston Head, the tower and ancillary buildings protected by a high-walled enclosure. To the west lies St. Adhelm's Head and Portland Bill; to the east the coast turns northwards to Swanage and Poole Bay. Completed in 1881, it was opened by the then Minister of Transport, Neville Chamberlain's father. The original illumination was by a paraffin vapour burner, followed by conversion to electricity in 1960. Anvil Point was finally automated in 1991.

˃ **Portland Bill, Dorset** The Isle of Portland is only just joined to the rest of Dorset by the end of the dramatic curve of shingle that is Chesil Beach. At the southernmost tip of this strange landscape of stone quarries and bleak villages is The Bill, a classic lighthouse of the imagination: a red and white striped tower on a rocky promontory. A little further inland are the old high and low lighthouses built in 1869. At 136 feet high, the tower is one of the tallest in Britain, displaying the protruding mouth of the now silent diaphone fog signal. The current light replaced them in 1905, standing even closer to the notorious race of agitated sea that tumbles between The Bill and the Shambles sandbank. On the very edge stands a tall white obelisk, an 1844 Trinity House seamark warning of a low, dangerous shelf of rock immediately below. It is not, as some have thought, a monument to Thomas Hardy.

the south west

^ **Berry Head, Brixham, Devon** Jackdaws scuffle about in the ivy-clad ruins of the disused fortifications built against possible French invasion in 1793, and 200 ft below, the heaving waters of the Brixham Roads move against the jagged rocks. At the end of this spectacular headland, the Berry Head light sits behind its iron railings amongst sea campion and wild dog roses. At this height there is no need for the light to be any taller, so the diminutive tower of 1906 is just the business end, converted to mains electricity only in 1994.

> **Fowey, Cornwall** John Betjeman, in his *Shell Guide to Cornwall* in 1965, wrote of Fowey that it was: '...a much visited place better seen by boat and on foot than by motor car.' Having been pressed against shop windows by 'visitors' with sunglasses on top of their heads driving Cherokee Jeeps, I can report that this observation is even more relevant today. Fowey is a waterside town – everything faces the river that winds down from Lostwithiel through steeply wooded slopes. This red tin man marks the point where the passenger ferry negotiates its way through the tugs and yachts across to Polruan.

← FERRY TO POLRUAN

< **St. Anthony's Head, Cornwall** An 1835 lighthouse that reveals itself very slowly. It appears to be so reluctant to show its face inland that its black chimneys look like a turned up collar. And quite rightly, for St. Anthony's business is seawards over the busy Carrick Roads, dividing the Roseland Peninsula from Falmouth. A navigational aid is needed here for vessels negotiating the Manacles rocks into Falmouth harbour, and in the late 18th century the Killigrew family flew a suitably large red flag from an elm tree. This romantic exhibition came to an end when its use could have equally aided an invading Napoleonic fleet.

∧ **Lizard, Cornwall** This is the most southerly point of mainland Britain, with the Lizard lighthouse guiding vessels in the English Channel and warning of the the offshore hazards of Lizard Point. Travelling down the long road from Helston, its distinctive twin towers connected by the row of keepers' cottages come into view after the village of Lizard itself. Only the north tower is now operational. In 1751 the towers were joined by a simple cottage in which an overlooker lay on a couch superintending the fires that provided the light. If they dimmed for any reason he sounded a cow horn to alert the bellows blowers of their duty.

The structure was altered to how we see it today in 1877 and included the engine room with a bay that houses the last operational compressed air fog signal, with twin black trumpets sprouting up from the roof. Warning is now emitted by a shrieking electric alternative attached to the railings of the light tower. In partnership with the Trevithick Trust, Trinity House opens the Lizard to the public, and you can see the fog signal preserved in full working order.

< The clock on the wall of the lantern room. One revolution of the smallest dial matches that of the lantern.

Trinity House National Lighthouse Centre, Penzance, Cornwall A tour of the lighthouses of Cornwall has to include this close-up experience of everything to do with maritime safety. If you drive around the coast road from Newlyn you can't miss it, as it advertises itself with marooned iron buoys in bright colours paraded on the forecourt. On this actual site over 100 years ago, the granite blocks for the Wolf Rock Tower were cut, and later it became a maintenance depot for the buoys. The floor is still made of the original rosewood blocks on which rest delights such as the gas-lit optic from Spurn Head, and two and a half tons of cut-glass light floating in three quarters of a ton of mercury from St. Mary's Island that can be set in motion by the touch of a finger. Very importantly, it houses a reconstruction of lighthouse living quarters, with curved furniture from Godrevy, a timely reminder that it is only recently that the human element was removed from every lighthouse in favour of automation.

< **Pendeen, Cornwall** I sat for a long time on a remote cliff top waiting for the mists to clear at Pendeen, my only company the occasional weeping sound of a seabird, the blast of the fog horn echoing around the headlands and extinct tin mine chimneys. Eerie fogs enshrouded the standing stones, crosses and fougou of West Penwith, just as they hid the inhospitable shore that stretches from the Pendeen Watch to St. Ives. This was a coast more familiar to the aftermaths of wrecks than any kind of positive prevention until the late 1890s, when the headland was flattened to receive the buildings we see today. A few primrose patches brighten the wastes of the keepers' gardens, as the deserted light sends telemetry signals across England to the Operational Control Centre on the Essex coast.

∨ **Godrevy, Cornwall** An exception to the rule about not being able to visit offshore lighthouses, as Godrevy is so close to the footpaths that wind through the thrift and heather of this St.Ives Bay peninsula. Close, but not close enough to escape the full force of Atlantic gales. In 1854 the steamer Nile was wrecked with the loss of all hands, and public and mercantile pressure resulted in an 85-foot-high octagonal tower being erected. The original optics were turned by clockwork driven by a large weight hanging down in the tower wall. Solar power has silently taken over.

^ **Hartland Point, Devon** The approach to Hartland Point is deceptive. One is lulled into a kind of clotted-cream security by quiet farmland crossed by hedgerows heavily scented with wild flowers, red campion and yellow buttercups tumbling from amongst green ferns into the lanes. And then, suddenly and abruptly, it all finishes. Pathways split open with giant gashes before disappearing altogether and red painted 'danger' signs proliferate on every convenient surface. Perseverance brings the Hartland lighthouse into view, peeping out from around the cone of gorse-strewn rock. It arrived here in 1874, a welcome guide for shipping approaching the Bristol Channel. Imagine being a child growing up here in this *Famous Five* storybook land, possibly your only companions the children of your father's three fellow keepers. Of course, your cottage would eventually be demolished to make way for a helicopter landing pad, but landing one of those here must be a nerve-wracking story all of its own.

< **Trevose Head, Cornwall** This was a dark corner of the North Cornwall coast until as late as 1847, when an oil light of wicks backed by reflectors was finally lit on the headland. Until this first flickering into life the only guiding lights were the Longships to the south and the old light on the island of Lundy to the north. The granite cliffs are forbidding, the rocks' razor-sharp surfaces slivered like oyster shells. The waves thunder into every crevice, their spent water flowing back into the turmoil like quicksilver. Until 1963 this atmosphere was aptly supplemented by Lord Rayleigh's monster fog horn blaring out over the seas from a 36-foot-long trumpet that sported an 18-foot-wide mouth.

Bull Point, Devon After all the wedding-cake architecture of most lighthouses, Bull Point comes as something of a shock. Built as the result of a landslip in September 1972, the base building is an adaptation of the 70s public lavatory style, but the squat light tower itself is fascinating. Placed around its circumference are giant oval concrete mouthpieces for the foghorns, the wonderfully named triple diaphones that last spoke in 1988.

ᴧ **Lynmouth Foreland, Devon** A lighthouse service road plunges down from the A39, negotiating tortuous hairpin bends where the last outcrops of Exmoor make their final descent into the sea. The landlord of a local inn still has waking nightmares of returning keepers down to their home on fogbound evenings. If you take care, the best approach is along the Somerset and North Devon Coast Path. Either way, the experience is exhilarating. The views are staggering and the lighthouse itself is a 1900 classic with a weather vane almost at eye level with the cottages above it on the precipitous slope.

Watchet, Somerset The way to arrive in Watchet is by the West Somerset Railway. This is where the line comes out of the western lee of the Quantocks and turns west at the sea to head for Minehead. The town is almost certainly where Samuel Taylor Coleridge talked with an old sea dog who became his inspiration for *The Rime of the Ancyent Marinere*. Now, the 'glittering eye' is the supremely economic harbour light on the jetty, a redcoat sentry with a gloriously swirling weathervane.

> **Beach lighthouse, Burnham-on-Sea,
> Somerset** A 19th-century curate had the idea
> of paying to turn Burnham into a spa town
> by extracting tolls from ships under passage
> to and from Bridgwater; this multi-legged
> structure was his marker. Those ships he
> managed to stop, paid for the sinking of trial
> wells that came to nothing. Now it serves
> more as a turning point for sand yachts
> racing down the beach from Berrow.

>> A previous light stands marooned amongst
> suburban gardens to the north of the town.

Blacknore Point, North Somerset Narrow strips of sand, seaweed, and dangerously soft black mud outline the Severn Estuary northwest of Bristol. The curious Blacknore light assists shipping moving in and out of the Avonmouth docks. Erected in 1894, its form suggests a Victorian's idea of a spacecraft, with braced and strutted cast-iron legs firmly planted in rock. Unless you're a local, the lighthouse is difficult to find, sitting on the edge of a Portishead suburb by a footpath following the shore. It was converted to automatic operation during the Second World War.

the north west

Fort Perch, New Brighton, Merseyside Fort Perch marks the northeastern extremity of the Wirral Peninsula. Here the ferries from Ireland and the Isle of Man making for the Mersey vie for attention with the amusement arcades and fairgrounds of New Brighton. The fort itself was built as protection for the port of Liverpool during the Napoleonic wars, but the foundation stone for the lighthouse was laid by Thomas Littledale, Mayor of Liverpool, in 1827. It is almost a direct copy of Smeaton's 18th-century Eddystone light. Now the 63-foot tower is a grey ghost standing perhaps as a sad reminder of the halcyon days when the great liners would have slid by in the final minutes of their voyages into Liverpool.

Ellesmere Port, Cheshire A simple brick lighthouse stands where the Shropshire Union Canal joins the Manchester Ship Canal. This access to the sea transformed Ellesmere over the years from a handful of rural villages into a giant oil port, along with petrol refineries and paper manufacturers. Much of this industry has gone, with Telford's handsome warehouses now scrubbed up as the Boat Museum, housing the world's largest collection of traditional canal boats. The light stands on the quay somewhat self-consciously, clean and spruce but shorn of its internal workings, adjusting to a new life as street furniture amongst the waterside flats and houses.

> **Fleetwood, Lancashire** Sir Peter Hesketh-Fleetwood founded this watering place and port in 1836 on the northern edge of his Fylde estate, overlooking Morecambe Bay. Docks, wharves and a railway that was once part of the only route from London to Scotland rapidly depleted his personal fortune. The town itself was planned, but never completed, by Decimus Burton, with streets radiating out like a fan, and included the design of these two wonderful lighthouses. The smaller of the two stands almost on the beach, with a balcony echoing Burton's Athenaeum Club in London.

∨ The other towers over the town, an 1840 pink sandstone column known as 'The Pharos' after the monumental light built off the harbour of Alexandria between 283 BC and 247 BC. It keeps a watchful eye on the goings-on at the bowling club below.

Cockersands, Lancashire A solitary, enchanting shore reached over quiet fields lying between the estuaries of the Cocker and Lune. The sea's edge is lined with only a handful of low-lying cottages and the battlemented sandstone remains of Cockersand Abbey, once a priory of the Premonstratensians (or the more pronounceable White Canons.) The eye is always drawn, however, to this little weathervaned sugar sifter sitting just in the waves. It marks the entrance to the Lune and Glasson Dock, a perfect antidote to the grey mass of the Heysham nuclear power station on the skyline.

< **St. Bees, Cumbria** Trinity House leased the first light here to Thomas Lutwige in 1718, for an annual rent of twenty pounds. His strong, round tower was topped by an iron grate into which coal was tipped by the equally strong keepers. Imagine performing this task as westerly winds howled over the 300-foot-high cliffs, and enduring the complaints of shipowners about the varying intensity of a light often shrouded in billowing black smoke. This filthy, cough-inducing practice continued until 1822, when, perhaps mercifully, the tower was destroyed by fire. One wonders how that happened. Oil took over in Joseph Nelson's new light seen here, making St. Bees the last coal-fired light in Britain.

∨ **Maryport, Cumbria** And so, on this windswept coast looking out to the hills of Galloway, our journey ends at Maryport. Here is Trinity House's most north western light, a plain aluminium beacon of 1996 vintage with an obscene message aerosoled in red paint on its side. As a sign of our times it is probably significant that 'pier' has been spelt 'pear'.

> More welcoming is the light of 1846, one of the oldest of its type. Its origins lie in a survey of this coast conducted in 1843 by Commander Denham RN, a marine surveyor. He discovered in Maryport that the only harbour light was a lamp placed in the window of Harbour House by a William Curry. Denham's report resulted in this iron beacon on its stone base on the south pier, looking like an adaptation of a Victorian clock tower from a stock catalogue.

acknowledgements I am indebted to Trinity House for their help and support, with particular thanks owed to Breda Wall and Jane Wilson. The website www.trinityhouse.co.uk gives information on all their operational lighthouses, and is essential reading for the technically minded. Anyone remotely interested in the subject should visit the absorbing Trinity House Lighthouse Centre in Penzance, and I am very grateful to Alan Renton there for his interest and help. My grateful thanks are also due to the following: At Everyman: David Campbell, Sandra Pisano and Clémence Jacquinet. At English Heritage: Val Horsler and Simon Bergin. At Anikst Design: Judith Ash and James Warner.

The National Trust, the Harbour Master's Office in Berwick-on-Tweed, John Stothert, Alan Adams at Redcar & Cleveland Borough Council, South Shields Library, Yorkshire Wildlife Trust, Ian Whitehead of the Hartlepool Arts & Museum Service, The Staghunters Inn at Brendon, the lady with the dog at Berry Head, the chaps at The Lizard, Fleetwood Bowling Club, Margaret Shepherd and Richard & Jane Gregory. For just about everything else, thanks are due to Elizabeth Raven-Hill.

bibliography *The Buildings of England Series*, Penguin Books. *The Shell County Guides*, Faber & Faber. *Lighthouses*, Lynn F. Pearson Shire Album 312, 1998. *Lost Sounds*, Alan Renton Whittles Publishing 2001.

The Lighthouse is a short story in *Seven by Five*, H.E.Bates, Michael Joseph 1963. *To the Lighthouse*, Virginia Woolf, The Hogarth Press 1927. The John Piper quotation is from *The Nautical Style* in *Buildings and Prospects*, The Architectural Press 1948. The Richard Jefferies quotation is from *The Breeze on Beachy Head* in *Nature near London* Chatto & Windus, The St. Martin's Library 1913.

‹ **Newlyn Harbour, Cornwall**

Overleaf:
Guy's Head, Sutton Bridge, Lincolnshire Another frequent visitor to the west lighthouse